Corner Grocery Store Principles

Seven Family Business Principles That Will Create Customers For Life

by
Joe Mangiaracina

Copyright 2023 Joe Mangiaracina. All rights reserved.

ISBN-13: (hardcover)
ISBN-13: (paperback)
ISBN-13: (ebook)
ISBN-13: (audiobook)

No part of this book may be reproduced in any form or by any electronic or mechanical means including information storage and retrieval systems, without permission in writing from the author. The only exception is by a reviewer, who may quote short excerpts in a review.

Although the author and publisher have made every effort to ensure that the information in this book was correct at press time, the author and publisher do not assume and hereby disclaim any liability to any party for any loss, damage, or disruption caused by errors or omissions, whether such errors or omissions result from negligence, accident, or any other cause.

This publication is designed to provide accurate and authoritative information with regard to the subject matter covered. It is sold with the understanding that the publisher is not engaged in rendering professional services. If legal advice or other expert assistance is required, the services of a competent professional should be sought.

The fact that an organization or website is referred to in this work as a citation and/or a potential source of further information does not mean that the author or the publisher endorses the information the organization or website may provide or recommendations it may make.

Please remember that Internet websites listed in this work may have changed or disappeared between when this work was written and when it is read.

AI Assist by Bookbud.ai

Cover page Designed by Get Covers

Table of Contents

Dedication 1

Introduction 4

Chapter 1: The Way Things Used to Be —
The Family-Owned Business 6

Chapter 2: The Family Business Mindset:
Building a Service Culture in Your Organization 9

Chapter 3: Deli Counter (Delivering
Products and Services One to One) 12

Chapter 4: The Produce Counter 16

Chapter 5: The Delivery Boy —
Employee/Owner Makes It Happen 19

Chapter 6: Bagging and Checkout — Paying for Value 24

Chapter 7: See Ya Next Week! 27

Chapter 8: Expanding Services: Growth for Growth's Sake? 30

Chapter 9: Keeping It in the Family 34

Chapter 10: When the Lights Go Out —
Crisis Management and Recovery 39

Chapter 11: Seasonal Changes —
Adapting and Innovating with the Times 42

Chapter 12: The Secret Recipe –
Sustaining Success Through Community Connection 45

Appendix A: Implementing Corner Grocery
Store Principles in Your Business 50

Appendix B: Acknowledgments.. 54

Dedication

This book is dedicated to my father who instilled in me a passion for service and appreciation and respect for customers from the time I was ten years old.

The familiar ring of a small bell as you push open an old wooden door. The scent of fresh bread, ripe tomatoes, and the honest sweat of hard work greets you before a warm, sincere "How can I help you?" fills the air. For those who've experienced it, there's immeasurable magic nestled in the corners of a family-owned grocery store. Such experiences aren't just transactions; they are relational touchstones that form the backbone of communities and the principles that can shape businesses for the better.

This book isn't just an operational guide; it's a heartfelt dedication to the values that have stood the test of time. It's a tribute to the mom-and-pop shops and family endeavors that keep the world turning on an axis of genuine care and personalized service. It's for the unsung heroes who know their customers by name, remember their kids' birthdays, and go out of their way to make each experience memorable.

The wisdom within these pages springs from the simple yet profound principles of service learned from my family's grocery store. It's not just a nostalgic trip down memory lane. It's a road map to embedding a customer-first attitude deep into the DNA of any organization, no matter the scale or industry. It's for you, the executive, the customer service leader, the visionary, who understands that excellence in service is both art and heart.

Let's face it, in an age where one click can replace an interaction with a human, there's something rebellious and daring about championing human connection. This book is penned with that rebellion in mind, inviting you to swim against the tide of faceless transactions and create spaces where customers don't just come and go—they belong.

You'll discover principles that might seem as outdated as the paper ledger, yet their effectiveness is undeniable, carving out remarkable experiences for those you serve. These are not just idealistic musings; they're the foundational strategies that have given life to powerhouse businesses, transforming mere transactions into unbreakable bonds of loyalty and mutual respect.

There's a spark lit behind every small gesture—be it the extra deli slice given "on the house" or the empathetic ear offered during a transaction. These sparks aren't quelled by scale or growth; they're fanned into flames when leaders like you champion them.

We will talk about principles that sound deceptively simple, like "Leaders Must Be Present and Accounted For" or "Do Whatever It Takes to Deliver the Goods". Yet, when practiced with conviction, these principles become transformative powers that elevate your business from the ordinary to the extraordinary.

This dedication to pre-digital era values in a hyper-digital world is an invitation to cultivate an environment where each team member from the top down understands the importance of a personal touch. It's an echo from the past that reverberates with timeless relevance, pushing you to ask not just 'What can we deliver?' but rather, 'How can we deliver it with care?'

From 'The Way Things Used to Be' to connecting 'The Secret Recipe' of community involvement, the ensuing chapters are an encouragement to weave strands of tradition into the fabric of modern business practices. This is not about resisting change but about retaining soul as you embrace it.

I dedicate these insights to the tireless entrepreneurs, the corner store owners, and the families who've nurtured their businesses through seasons of change. Their tenacity, love, and wisdom have inspired this narrative, aimed at enriching your business philosophy and, in turn, your customer's experience.

Remember, business isn't just a matter of profit and margins; it's a matter of people and moments. It's recognizing that there will always be a demand for the warm and the genuine amidst the cold and the instant. It's about aligning your company's heartbeat with the very customers who keep it alive.

As we embark together on this journey through each chapter, keep your mind open to the quiet yet potent power of customer intimacy, of service done not just well, but with passion and personalization. Embrace these principles as if your own family's name were above your business's door, because when you boil it down, isn't that the signature of any truly great company?

The greatest dedication we can make is to honor those timeless virtues: hard work, integrity, and service with a smile. It's marveling at the wisdom of generations past and using it as a guiding star in the sky of modern business. This book, this journey, is dedicated to those principles and to you, the leaders who keep them alive. May their light lead you to excellence.

Let's roll up our sleeves and make our businesses not just places of trade, but homes of heart. Let's write stories of service that aren't recounted in transaction logs but enshrined in the memories of those we serve. Together, let's redefine what it means to be in business—and in service—in today's world.

Introduction

Imagine walking into a place where the aroma of freshly baked bread dances through the air, where each product on the shelf has a story, and the smile greeting you is as genuine as the age-old wooden floors creaking underfoot. This book isn't about that idyllic past alone, it's about bringing the heart and soul of my family's grocery store into the fast-paced world of modern business. It's about translating those simple, yet powerful, principles that can make any customer interaction truly memorable, no matter the size of your company.

You might run a multinational corporation, lead a customer service team, or manage a bustling department – but the essence of great customer service remains unchanged. It's about seeing your business through the eyes of that family-owned grocery store, where every detail mattered because every customer mattered. We're embarking on a journey to rediscover the value of presence, flexibility, commitment, and connection – values that turn first-time buyers into lifelong patrons. It's these values that we'll explore, principles grounded in the realities of day-to-day business operations but inspired by the timeless charm of a corner grocery store.

Through the pages of this book, you'll find insights and strategies infused with a passion for excellence and a dedication to service that can transform the customer experience your organization offers. These are the lessons that have stood the test of time, that have propelled businesses to the forefront of their industries, and that have engraved their brand names in the hearts of their customers. So, as we step forward, let's weave the wisdom of yesterday into the fabric of today's enterprises, creating customer experiences that aren't just satisfactory but are truly extraordinary.

Chapter 1:
The Way Things Used to Be —
The Family-Owned Business

As we turn the corner from the introduction, we delve into the golden era of the family-owned business, a time when personal relationships ruled and a handshake was as good as a written contract. My own journey in mastering customer experience didn't start in the boardroom. It began in a family-owned grocery store, where fresh produce wasn't just about fruits and vegetables; it was about the fresh approach to each customer that walked through the door.

The heart of this story isn't stuck in some bygone era; it's very much alive, living in those of us who remember the art of true service. In that little store, we learned that every interaction was an opportunity to build a lasting relationship. A smile, a genuine conversation, and the anticipation of a customer's needs were our daily bread — both literally and metaphorically.

When you entered, you weren't just another face in the queue; you were Mary who loved ripe tomatoes or John who had a penchant for artisanal cheeses. Knowing your customers, understanding not just what they bought but why they bought it, was essential. This wasn't just to sell more. It was the foundation upon which trust and loyalty were built.

Consider this: in a time without social media, every satisfied customer became a living, breathing testimonial to the next. Exceptional service wasn't just 'nice to have,' it was our lifeblood. It meant the difference between thriving or just surviving, for in a family business, every dollar mattered and every customer was a pillar of your success.

Let's not gloss over the fact that it wasn't all sunshine and rainbows. Running a family business had its share of challenges. However, those hurdles never stopped the unwavering commitment to serve. We had to innovate within our means, taking personal responsibility for the experience we provided. This drive shapes my perspective to this day, arguing that heart, hustle, and a dedication to service can elevate any company, regardless of its size.

There was a simple magic in the way things used to be. That magic was the underpinning of a business philosophy that saw customers as the northern star. Yes, family businesses relied on instinct and hard work, but they also thrived on the soft skills that sometimes get lost in today's efficiency-driven metrics. They understood that business isn't about B2B or B2C, it's about P2P — people to people.

The family-owned grocery store of yesterday can't compete with today's hypermarkets in terms of scale, but it can certainly school them in the finesse of customer experience. And it's this same finesse that can, and should, be infused into today's corporate mammoths.

Embedding these principles into modern businesses is not just about nostalgia. It's about creating a competitive advantage that can't be easily replicated. You can imitate a product, undercut prices, or mimic an ad campaign, but the genuine warmth and personalized service of a mom-and-pop shop? That's a tougher act to follow.

Stick with me as we embark on a journey that takes these age-old truths and integrates them into your executive toolkit. Every principle here comes with the promise to not just meet but exceed customer expectations. We're not going to reinvent the wheel; we're going to make it spin with the same passion and commitment that powered the family-owned grocery stores of yesteryear.

By the time we close this chapter, I want you to grasp the spirit of those times and understand that the very essence of phenomenal service is timeless. It rests in the small gestures, the extra mile, and the recognition that behind every transaction is a human interaction that holds the potential for greatness. Let's bring back that heartbeat of business, pulse by pulse, customer by customer.

Chapter 2:
The Family Business Mindset: Building a Service Culture in Your Organization

In our family's grocery store, one fundamental truth was held above all: the way we serve is as vital as what we serve. Let's unpack what it really takes to embed that ethos into the DNA of your organization. Think of it not merely as a duty to your customers, but as a cherished family tradition that delivers unparalleled value both to them and to your business.

A service culture doesn't appear out of thin air. It's crafted with intention, ingrained by leaders, and nurtured by every member of the team. Picture your company as a complex tapestry; every employee is a thread contributing to the overall image. When one thread falters, the entire tapestry can be compromised. That's why instilling a sense of ownership and pride in each individual is pivotal to fostering a thriving service culture.

Building a service culture requires us to look beyond transactions to the very core of human interaction. In the family grocery store, each customer interaction was an opportunity to cement a relationship—knowing customers by name, remembering their favorite products, and even asking about their families. It's this personal touch that transforms a simple exchange into a meaningful encounter.

Leadership must not only set the example but be actively involved in the cultivation of this culture. Being present isn't just about showing up; it's about being genuinely engaged with your employees and customers, making them feel heard, and appreciated. It's about demonstrating that service isn't just a department, it's the entirety of your business expressed in every action and decision.

Moreover, empowering your team is essential. Empowerment breeds confidence, and confident employees don't just follow procedures—they go above and beyond because they care deeply about the outcome. They become the embodiment of your service culture because they have a stake in it.

Training plays a crucial part, too. Think of it as continual relationship-building—not just between your staff and the customers, but within the organization itself. Cultivating a team that communicates effectively, supports one another, and feels comfortable to take initiative is key to making each customer feel they are part of something special.

Feedback—both giving and receiving—is the lifeblood of continuous improvement. Encouraging open lines of communication not only helps nip problems in the bud but also celebrates successes. It's all about creating an environment where the goal is not to avoid mistakes but to learn and grow from them together as a family would.

Let's not forget, a service culture has a ripple effect. Customers who experience genuine service become not just patrons but advocates for your brand. And happy employees tend to deliver better service, which in turn leads to increased customer satisfaction, and ultimately, loyalty. It's a positively reinforcing cycle that starts with you setting the service culture standard.

Intrinsically, a servile mindset is less about policies and more about principles. It's about viewing every request as an opportunity, every complaint as a gift, and every day as a chance to leave a lasting impression. It's a choice to build a legacy of extraordinary service that stands the test of time, regardless of your industry or market changes.

Consider this chapter a compass guiding you towards creating and sustaining a service culture that resonates with the warmth and dedication of a family business. A service culture isn't just a facet of your operation; it's the heart from which every interaction pumps lifeblood. So, take this to heart, bake it into every level of your organization, and watch as the seeds of exceptional service blossom into long-term success.

CORNER GROCERY STORE PRINCIPLE #1:

"Leaders Must Be Present and Accounted For" embodies the simple truth that genuine, unwavering customer attention is the foundation of any thriving business, just as knowing each patron's name and needs was central to our family corner store's success.

In our humble corner grocery, the owner was always a handshake away, eyes sparkling with the day's challenge. Picture this image in your corporate hallways, in the lobby, by the water cooler—your leaders as the lifeblood, the heartbeat of action and decision-making. They're not some distant figureheads, but rather, active players on the front lines, deeply involved in the dance of day-to-day operations. They know their presence fuels the fire of inspiration, stokes the engine of productivity, and builds a fortress of trust with every employee and customer alike. Their footsteps on the shop floor, their genuine interest in their team's tasks, their on-the-spot decisions—it's this visceral leadership that turns the ordinary into extraordinary, infusing a spirit of excellence in service that's felt in every interaction. Your leaders must be more than just a name on a door; they've got to be present, fully with you, there shoulder-to-shoulder, because that's how you create a company culture that's as rich, engaging, and irresistible as the smell of fresh bread wafting from your neighborhood bakery.

Chapter 3:
Deli Counter (Delivering Products and Services One to One)

Continuing from the ethos of a family business, we enter the domain of direct, personal service akin to what you experience at a deli counter. Envision this: as you approach the counter, you're not just another customer in line; you represent a unique set of preferences and expectations that the person behind the counter must identify and fulfill with precision. This is where the art of delivering products and services on an individual basis comes into sharp focus.

Imagine a scenario where every slice of ham is a bespoke solution. Your deli attendant asks you, "How would you like it sliced?" and this seemingly simple question encapsulates the essence of personalized service - adaptability. Just like the thickness of a slice of cheese that can be tailored to customer preference, your services must be calibrated to the unique needs and desires of each individual who walks through your doors.

Now, let's translate this into corporate terms. Behind the 'Deli Counter' of your business, your employees are the frontline attendants, serving up your products and services. They must listen carefully, respond attentively, and tailor each experience like they're adjusting the slicer - being nimble and adaptable to every customer's request. This is the cornerstone of creating memorable interactions that resonate with your clientele. It's a shift from a one-size-fits-all approach to an individualized, customer-centric strategy.

Corner Grocery Store Principles

Delivering one to one means understanding the nuances that turn a satisfactory experience into an extraordinary one. Sometimes, it's about going the extra mile - much like when a deli clerk spots a regular reaching the front of the line and, without prompting, starts preparing their usual order. In your businesses, this could translate into anticipating your clients' needs, perhaps by providing proactive support before an issue even arises or by tailoring a product presentation to align with their previous purchasing patterns.

What further sets the deli counter model apart is the immediacy of feedback. Watch closely the face of a customer sampling a slice of salami. Is it too salty? Too dry? In the same instant, make the necessary adjustments. In your operation, encourage open dialogues with customers. Let them know their voices are not only heard but also heeded. Make agility a hallmark of your service - it's not about being flawless but about mastering the ability to adjust swiftly and smoothly when something isn't quite right.

Call it intuition or call it acute customer observation, but the ability to deliver products and services one to one is much about reading between the lines. A customer's offhand comment or body language can tell you much about their needs - listen to what's not being said just as acutely as you would their direct request. When your teams master this, they transcend mere service providers; they become customer-experience artists.

Nevertheless, individualized service isn't just about the feel-good factor; it triggers a ripple effect. Delighted customers become your evangelists; they tout your brand not because they've been asked to but because they genuinely want to share their exceptional experience. And isn't that the mark of a business truly thriving?

Shifting gears back to you, the leaders, the ethos of the 'Deli Counter' resides in giving your team autonomy - entrust them to make judgment calls that best serve the customer in the moment. This doesn't undermine the importance of policies and procedures but emphasizes the need for a balance wherein employees feel empowered to act with the customer's best interest at heart.

Remember, while we can automate many things in business, we can't automate genuine human connection. There's an irreplaceable value in the warmth of a smile, the empathy in a voice, and the assurance of a human touch. Our world is moving constantly towards hyper-efficiency, but let's never lose sight of the power of one-to-one service, where every encounter is treated as a unique opportunity to make a lasting impression.

As we wrap up this chapter, think of your business's product and service delivery as the most dynamic deli counter in town. Keep the lines of customer communication open, be flexible, and provide individualized solutions that leave your customers feeling valued and understood. You're not just serving products or services; you're providing an experience - one that, if crafted well, will have them coming back for more.

CORNER GROCERY STORE PRINCIPLE #2:

"Thick or Thin, Flexibility Is In" Embrace the mindset that customer preferences vary like the many cuts of cold cuts at the deli—flexibility in meeting their needs isn't just nice, it's necessary.

This resonating mantra from the deli counter is not just about slicing cold cuts to customer preference; it's a metaphor for the adaptability that every business leader must embrace. When running a family-owned grocery store, you quickly learn that no two customers are the same, and their needs can change as fast as the weather. One day, a customer wants their ham sliced so thin it could almost float away, and the next, they're looking for a hearty thick-cut to anchor their family meal. Flexibility isn't just nice to have; it's a necessity, and it's what keeps customers coming through the door.

Now, let's translate that to any business context. As executives and customer service leaders, imagine if you were as responsive to your clients as a family grocer is to their patrons. It means tuning in to the subtle shifts in demands, preferences, and market trends — and not being afraid to tailor your approach accordingly. Flexible policies might very well be your competitive edge, allowing you to pivot faster than larger, more rigid competitors. It starts with adopting a mindset that every interaction is an opportunity to demonstrate value by bending without breaking, all in the service of customer satisfaction.

Being flexible doesn't mean compromising on quality or core values; it means being open to finding new pathways to deliver that value. It's about looking beyond the 'one-size-fits-all' solution and crafting experiences that resonate on a personal level. Sure, standardization is great for efficiency, but customization breeds loyalty. A company that can do both — that balances efficiency with personalized service — is hitting the sweet spot of business agility. It's not enough to simply 'meet expectations' anymore; we must strive to exceed them with a nimbleness that keeps us one step ahead. In the ever-evolving dance of business, flexibility ensures that you're always in step with the music, ready to adapt your rhythm at a moment's notice.

Chapter 4:
The Produce Counter

As you've journeyed with us through the intricacies of the corner grocery store, you've likely begun to appreciate the nuances that make a family-owned business tick. Now let's turn to the produce counter—I see it as an analogy for treating your customers with the care and attention they deserve. Take, for instance, a ripe peach. It demands to be handled with tenderness, less it bruises. Our customers, just like that peach, often seek a gentle touch, an understanding nod, or a warm smile. Then there's the humble potato—robust, less delicate, but still needing attention to keep it in prime condition. Your business approach needs to adapt to the individual needs of each customer, just as you would handle each piece of produce with the care that its unique characteristics demand.

It's not enough to push products or services at your clients; it's essential that you understand them. You ought to know their preferences, their dislikes, who they're buying for, and what makes them return. Are they looking for the freshest, organic produce or the budget-friendly buys that help stretch their dollar? Are you attending to them through a custom hand-selection service or offering the convenience and speed they require? Just as in our store, where we learned to read the nuances in a shopper's behavior at the produce counter, so must you discern these preferences in your clientele.

This understanding is the cornerstone of corner grocery store principle number three. It's a humorous metaphor, sure, but it underscores a vital truth. Not every client will respond well to the same approach, and it's your task—as it is ours with produce—to identify what handling each customer requires for a truly exceptional service experience. In doing so, you recognize their individuality, which breeds loyalty and trust. It might seem daunting at first, but think about this: if you can successfully handle a ripe tomato without a single bruise, imagine how your customized care can impress your clients.

And, just like the ever-changing selection of produce that varies from season to season, you need to expect and respond to the evolving needs and tastes of your customers. Keep your ear to the ground, and when you spot trends or sense a shift in the market, don't be afraid to switch up your offerings. The dynamism of the produce counter demands it—it's a lively, colorful dance of supply, demand, and desire. Translate that energy into your interactions with your clients. Feed them fresh ideas regularly and watch as their eyes light up at your latest offering, just like a child eyeing the first strawberries of summer.

Lastly, remember that the produce counter is more than just a transactional space—it's a hub of conversation, advice, and relationship building. Encourage your team to engage with clients, share insights, and connect beyond the sale. Your customers aren't just buying a product; they're seeking an experience that they can't find with your competitors. Make every moment count, from hello to thank you. Harness the living, breathing essence of the produce counter, and inject it into every interaction. In the end, it's these connections that will keep your clients coming back for more. After all, who doesn't want to shop where they're treated not just as another sale, but as a part of the family?

CORNER GROCERY STORE PRINCIPLE #3:

"Treat Your Customer Like a Fruit or Vegetable. Just Make Sure You Know the Difference" reminds us that understanding and catering to the individual needs of our customers is akin to distinguishing between the care of fruits and vegetables; it's all about recognizing the nuances that ensure we handle each interaction with the appropriate touch.

Welcome to the produce counter, where the scent of fresh produce embodies the crisp satisfaction of superb customer service. In this vibrant space, great attention is given to understanding the nuances of fruits and vegetables, just as we should with our customers. Imagine treating a tomato like a head of lettuce; the result would be disastrous! Similarly, business leaders need keen insights to discern the subtle needs and preferences of each customer.

Each fruit and vegetable requires unique care—bananas need hanging to avoid bruising, while potatoes are best kept in cool, dark spaces. Our customers are no different. Some demand regular check-ins and personal interactions, craving the sunlight of your attention. Others prefer a less hands-on approach, much like a cactus, thriving with minimal care but still expecting high-quality service. The wisdom lies in recognizing that one-size-fits-all doesn't work in a produce section or in customer service. By observing and responding to the individuality of your customers, tailoring service to their specific needs, you can nurture robust relationships that keep them coming back for more.

Let's consider how you can apply this in your role as a leader. Take the time to learn your customers' preferences, just as you would study the care tags for various produce. Engage with your team to develop an eye for these details, ensuring that each interaction creates a customer experience as delightful as the perfect peach on a summer day. The lesson of the tomato and the lettuce is simple but profound: when you truly understand and respect the individuality of your clientele and respond accordingly, you cultivate a customer experience that is both memorable and fruitful—and that's the kind of exceptional service that leads to growth, both for your customers and your business.

Chapter 5:
The Delivery Boy —
Employee/Owner Makes It Happen

Imagine a young delivery boy, weaving his bike through busy city streets, just to ensure that your groceries reach your doorstep in time for dinner. That vivid image captures the heart of what it takes to deliver exceptional customer service. The tenacity and responsibility that this delivery boy embodies is precisely the spirit that must permeate every level of your organization. It's all about adopting that employee/owner mindset: taking ownership of each task as if the success of the entire company hinges upon it, because, in many ways, it does.

In the tapestry of our family-owned grocery store's operations, the delivery boy wasn't just a cog in the machine; he was as essential as the grocer selecting the freshest produce or the cashier's warm smile. Every person understood that their role was pivotal. The same principle applies to every business striving for excellence. When you empower your team to act and feel like owners, they become invested in the outcome, they innovate, they handle challenges proactively, they go the extra mile — they do whatever it takes to deliver the goods.

Yet, it's not just about personal responsibility. It's about cultivating an environment where each employee feels trusted and valued. This means providing the tools, the training, and the trust that enables them to act decisively. When they spot an issue, they shouldn't just pass it up the chain — they should feel confident in addressing it then and there. It's about creating 'owners' across all levels of your organization who feel that their contributions are making a direct impact.

Take it from our delivery boy — obstacles were merely opportunities for him to demonstrate his dedication. This can-do attitude is contagious, and it starts at the top. Executives and leaders must model the behavior they want to see. Celebrate those who take initiative. Praise the problem-solvers. Reward the employees who embody the very essence of ownership. This recognition fuels a culture that perpetuates positive action and exceptional service.

But why does this matter? Because today's customers have a plethora of choices at their fingertips, and what sets you apart isn't just your product but the service and the overall experience your team delivers. An employee who takes ownership creates a customer experience that resonates, that feels personalized and genuine, and that builds loyalty. This is how you transform one-time buyers into lifetime advocates for your brand.

In an era where everyone's looking for a shortcut or a hack, the employee/owner approach is honest work. It's rolling up your sleeves, it's getting into the trenches, it's showing up every day with the resolve to make things happen. It's the delivery boy, through rain or sleet, making sure that what was promised is what's received — no excuses.

The true value of this mentality isn't just in the big heroic moments; it's in the small, everyday actions. It's the call center employee staying on the line an extra few minutes to ensure complete resolution of an issue, the project manager who reworks the schedule to meet an urgent client deadline, or the maintenance crew that fixes a problem before most are even aware it exists. Each action might seem insignificant in isolation, but collectively, they are the bedrock of your business's reputation.

To build this sense of ownership, communication is crucial. Employees at every level should understand how their day-to-day work directly affects the company's goals. They need to see the big picture and their unique role within it. This clarity fosters a sense of purpose and meaning in their work, which in turn, inspires them to go above and beyond the standard expectations.

Operational systems and policies must support this entrepreneurial spirit, not stifle it. Flexibility in processes allows employees to make judgement calls that align with customer satisfaction goals without becoming mired in red tape. Remember that innovation often comes from those on the front lines, so give them the latitude to experiment and provide feedback. That's how your business stays nimble and inventive, just like that delivery boy finding new shortcuts on his route.

Chapter 5 isn't just a nostalgic look back at a simpler time; it's a potent reminder that the success of any business hinges on the people who own their roles within it. It's a call to foster the employee/owner mind-set. So encourage it, nurture it, reward it. Because when your team delivers with the heart of an owner, your customers will notice, and your business will thrive.

CORNER GROCERY STORE PRINCIPLE #4:

"Do Whatever It Takes to Deliver the Goods" shows us that the essence of exceptional service is embodied by an employee's drive to 'Do Whatever It Takes to Deliver the Goods,' ensuring customers leave not just satisfied, but thrilled and eager to return.

This principle is the force that drives every memorable customer service experience. It's the unyielding commitment to go the extra mile, no matter what. And let me tell you, in the heyday of our family grocery store, we knew the importance of taking that extra step; it was what separated us from the competing chains that treated customers as just another number. We knew our customers by name, knew their families, and understood deeply that to keep our community flourishing, we had to ensure the delivery of not just goods, but excellence.

Think about it - when you promise a customer that a product will arrive by a certain time, you're not just sending out an item, you're sending out a tacit guarantee of your service. If it means staying late to oversee that the delivery truck doesn't miss its window or navigating through a storm to ensure that promise is kept, then so be it. That's the ethos that should run through the veins of every team member, from the C-suite to the front desk. This isn't about being heroes; this is about being dedicated professionals who understand the value of keeping a promise.

What "doing whatever it takes" also means is having a plan B... and a plan C, D, and E if necessary. It's about anticipation and ready responses for when things don't go as planned. It could be anything from a sudden product shortage to a system outage. What do you do? You improvise, you adapt, and you overcome. You secure your supply chains, train your teams to handle crises, and create contingencies that will hold even when the unexpected hits. Because in the end, your customers don't necessarily remember what went wrong, they remember how you fixed it.

But remember, "doing whatever it takes" isn't about reckless decisions or cutthroat tactics; it's about being resourceful and responsible. It's about ethical ingenuity. We're not just delivering a product - we're upholding a trust that our customers have placed in us, and sometimes, we're part of critical supply lines in their lives. We make sure we're not just meeting expectations but exceeding them, because that is what builds enduring relationships and brand loyalty.

Bringing this principle to life requires a consistent organizational mindset, starting from leadership. As executives and customer service leaders, our task is to instill this critical value into the fabric of our business culture, train our teams to embody it, and lead by example. We must inspire and motivate, not dictate. When your entire organization breathes this commitment, the result is a reliable, resilient, and remarkable service to every customer, every time.

Chapter 6:
Bagging and Checkout — Paying for Value

The conclusion of the shopping experience—where goods are bagged and transactions are completed—represents a crucial inflection point in customer service and satisfaction. It's where the value that has been promised is finally exchanged for the price that's been set. Just as the bagging and checkout counters are where we ensure customers leave satisfied with their physical purchases in hand, in any organizational context, this phase is where we ensure the customer perceives and understands the value they're receiving.

Picture a well-executed checkout process: It's not just about handing over items; it's the final opportunity to validate the customer's choice in their purchases. When the cashier asks, "Did you find everything okay?" or "Were you happy with your shopping experience today?" they're reinforcing the notion that the customer's satisfaction is the store's top priority. The customer should leave feeling not just like they've completed a transaction, but like they've made the right decision in investing their time and resources with your company. This level of care in the checkout process can transform a mundane purchase into a reaffirmation of value.

Payment marks an implicit contract between the business and the customer. It's not just money for products—it's money for service, for experience, for trust. Customers pay for the value they perceive, and their perception of this value can last long beyond when the money has changed hands. That's why ensuring they grasp the inherent worth of what they're buying is essential. This is not just about the innate quality of the product, but also about the wrap-around service, the smiles, and the human touchpoints that colour the entirety of their engagement with your business.

So, how do you ensure the customer is recognizing this value at that final, critical moment? Transparency is key. Itemized receipts that are clear and detailed show customers exactly what they're paying for, which, in turn, reinforces the value of each item or service provided. Even when discussing service-based industries, the metaphor stands strong; billing and invoicing should be equally transparent, serving to gently remind the customer of the benefits they've received or will continue to enjoy.

Don't forget about the 'baggers'—those who carefully place customers' purchases into bags, ready to be taken home. In the broader business sense, these are the employees who deliver the end product to the customer. Their role in ensuring the safe and neat packaging of a customer's items cannot be overstated. They need to be as detail-oriented and as customer-focused as the business demands. They are also responsible for that last impression, making sure the product leaves the business as perfectly as it was promoted and sold.

This stage is, furthermore, ripe for solidifying customer loyalty. Loyalty programs can be beneficial if leveraged in the right manner. Think beyond the points and discounts—consider providing useful information, tips, or complementary services that extend the value of the purchase. For instance, suggest recipes for the ingredients a customer buys or offer maintenance tips for acquired electronics. It's about providing additional benefits that serve to both increase customer enjoyment and cement the relationship between the buyer and your brand.

Additionally, flexibility and efficiency at checkout can't be overlooked. Mobile payment options, self-checkout, and multiple payment platforms—it's all about convenience for the customer. This doesn't just provide ease—it communicates that you value the customer's time as much as they do. It addresses the modern-day desire for speed without sacrificing the personal touch we've emphasized.

Lastly, an expressive and sincere 'thank you' can make all the difference. It's surprising how these two simple words can affect customer retention. A genuine expression of gratitude for a customer's business acknowledges that their spending is more than a transaction; it's a choice to trust and engage with your brand.

As leaders and customer service champions, it's our duty to ensure that the paying process is just as enriching as the shopping process. It's where every touchpoint comes full circle, and where the final impression is made. It's a reminder that every interaction is a chance to affirm the customer's decision to engage with us, and a well-honed checkout process truly pays off in customer satisfaction and loyalty.

In crafting a checkout experience that highlights the worth of what's on offer, you're doing much more than wrapping up a sale. You're fortifying a relationship. You're making it clear that when customers choose to engage with you, they're receiving full value—and then some—for their expenditure. Cause let's face it, in the end, we're not just in the business of selling products or services. We're in the business of selling experiences, and those experiences better be worth every penny.

Chapter 7:
See Ya Next Week!

Ever noticed the warm invitation back, at the end of a satisfying encounter at a local store? That's not just a pleasantry; it's the sound of a relationship being nurtured and the seed of loyalty being planted. In the heart of our family's grocery, this wasn't just a farewell, it was a pledge – a promise that we'd be right there waiting to offer an experience just as stellar, or better, the next time around. In your business, whether it's within the corporate offices or the vibrant hum of customer service departments, ensuring that every customer interaction ends with a subconscious bookmark that brings them back is golden.

Think about it, when someone walks away from your product or service, they carry with them an impression that could turn into a storyteller's tale. And you want that story to have the kind of ending that makes the audience say, "I want to be part of that story." That's why every customer interaction needs to be not just a transaction but an installment in an ongoing saga of stellar service and unforgettable experiences. Your customers don't just walk out with a product or service; they leave with a feeling, an expectation, and if you've played your cards right, an anticipation for what's next.

Securing that 'See Ya Next Week!' is less about the parting words and more about what's built before that. When customers feel valued, understood, and pleasantly surprised, they don't just come back; they look forward to it. That anticipation becomes a part of their routine, their conversations, and before you know it, your brand is part of their lifestyle. This is how a single visit can evolve into a tradition, flourishing into what every business covets the most – lifetime customer value.

The brilliance of this concept lies not in complex strategies but in genuine gestures, consistency, and the kind of authenticity that can't be fabricated. Remember that how we make people feel is far more memorable than what we sell them. Are they just another number in the monthly sales report, or are they the cherished neighbor whose name the entire staff knows by heart? Turning a momentary engagement into a long-term relationship is part art, part science, but all heart.

So, as you flip through the pages of your own company's story, pause at each chapter's end and ask yourself, "Will our customers be eager for the next chapter?" Make sure your business is the one they can't wait to return to, ensuring every encounter ends not with a silent farewell but with a resonant, 'See Ya Next Week!'

Lifetime Customer Value embodies the heart and soul of a thriving business, much like the subtle yet undeniable vitality of the family-owned grocery store that knows every patron by name. This concept is not only about sales; it's about the relationships and the accumulated benefits of nurturing them. Imagine a customer, let's call her "Evelyn," who's been coming to your store every Thursday for the past twenty years. She isn't just purchasing groceries; she's building a story, a history with your business. The threads of loyalty and trust that stretch over two decades are not forged through transactions alone but through the smiles, the small chats, and the personalized service she gets every time she visits.

The magic of Lifetime Customer Value grows exponentially when you realize that Evelyn is likely sharing her experiences with friends and family. Making her not only a customer but also an ambassador. She represents a relationship that's worth potentially thousands of dollars more than her individual purchases might suggest. In business, we must perceive this value as a holistic measure, a living testament to the saying, 'You reap what you sow.' By plowing resources into ensuring every Evelyn out there feels valued, heard, and appreciated, you're cultivating a fertile garden of lifetime patrons, a heritage of supporters who will weather economic ups and downs with you.

In essence, Lifetime Customer Value is about viewing each customer as an evolving partnership rather than a static revenue source. It's recognizing that every positive interaction adds layers to a foundation that will support both your customer's and your business's future growth. Invest in these partnerships, because a single seed of loyalty, planted in the fertile soil of exceptional service, carries with it the potential to grow into a towering tree, casting a wide shadow that attracts new life and opportunities beneath its branches. This understanding bridges the gap from pure transaction to genuine connection—the bedrock of sustaining a flourishing enterprise in any industry.

Chapter 8:
Expanding Services: Growth for Growth's Sake?

As we look back at the history woven through the passages of our family's grocery store, there's an unmistakable pattern of growth intertwined with an unwavering commitment to service. But let's pause for a moment to consider: in the world of business expansion, is adding services and growing the company footprint always the right move? It's tempting to equate business growth with success. However, the savvy leader is one who asks, "Am I growing for a purpose, or just for the sake of growth?"

Growth should never dilute what made you distinctive and beloved in the first place. When you decide to expand your services, it's like planting new seeds in your garden. You have to tend to them, ensuring they're nurtured, but without neglecting the flourishing plants that have sustained your garden thus far. It's a delicate balance between watering the new and fertilizing the old. This is when your core value proposition becomes your North Star, guiding your expansion in alignment with your values and mission.

The goal should always be to enhance, not overshadow, the unique experience your customers have come to expect from you. Sometimes, growth can sneak up and tip the scales, causing a once-customer-centric business to become an empire that's lost its personal touch. Remember, every time you add a new service or department, you're not just offering something new; you're inviting your customers to place their trust in this extension of your brand. It's essential to ask yourself whether this new branch will strengthen or weaken that trust.

Growth must be strategic, yes, but it should also be sustainable. It's about reinforcing the foundation, not just adding extra floors to an already swaying structure. As you consider expanding services, keep circling back to your raison d'être. What is the purpose behind this addition? Will it genuinely benefit your customers, or is it just a shiny new offering that looks good on paper? Expansion should feel less like inflating a balloon and more like building out a robust framework – one that can stand firm amid the winds of change and competition.

Ultimately, as leaders and pioneers in our field, we must recognize that growth is not just numerical—it's experiential. Our drive to expand should be rooted in elevating the experience, not just enlarging the enterprise. It's the difference between growing a brand customers recognize and nurturing one they love. Our family's grocery store stood the test of time and grew into a flourishing catering business because we understood that growth, when done with purpose and care, can enrich both our business and our customers' lives. Let's ensure we keep that wisdom at the heart of our future plans.

How to Retain That Small Company Feel While Growing Your Business Scaling up doesn't mean losing the intimate, personal touch that made your business stand out in the first place. Remember, at the heart of any successful expansion is the ability to maintain the essence of what brought you initial acclaim. As your organization grows, keep layers of bureaucracy to a minimum. This isn't just talk; this is about fostering an environment where everyone from the CEO to the newest recruit feels approachable and connected. Encourage leadership to spend time on the front lines, to understand both employees' and customers' experiences firsthand. Transparency and open lines of communication aren't just feel-good policies; they're strategic advantages that can tip the scales in your favor.

Don't let robust growth dilute the personalization of your services. That attentive clerk who remembers a customer's name isn't a quaint vestige of the past, it's a pillar of future success. Invest in training your team to value each customer interaction as an opportunity to leave a memorable impression. As the number of your customer interactions grows, leverage technology to provide personalized experiences at scale. Use data to understand preferences, but never let the human touch fall by the wayside. The balance here is critical; technology supports the personal touch, it does not replace it.

Lastly, celebrate your heritage enthusiastically and often. Your story is magnetic, and it's what pulls people in. As you expand, don't shy away from sharing where you came from and why you're passionate about what you do. Hold onto the traditions that spell out your identity and never lose sight of your roots. When customers and employees feel they are part of something bigger, part of a story, they'll help carry the culture with them as they embrace the growth around them. Keep it real, keep it familiar, and keep it close to your core – that's how you'll retain that small company feel while reaching for the stars.

Sticking with Your Core Value Proposition As we unpack the essence of your business, let's hone in on what really sets you apart: your core value proposition. It's this nave to which the spokes of your business wheel are attached, it's what your customers come for and keep coming back for. In the melodic rhythm of everyday business, there's often the temptation to chase new trends or add services that deviate from the heart of what you do. However, staying true to your core promise isn't just about keeping a tight focus, it's about excelling in the very thing you've told your customers they can rely on you for.

Imagine our family's grocery store deciding one day to sell furniture. We might catch a few glances, perhaps even make a few unexpected sales. But what happens when our regulars come in for the fresh produce and congenial atmosphere we're known for, only to find couches cluttering the aisles? Confusion. Dilution of brand identity. And worst of all, a detracted focus from our expertise in offering the freshest, most delectable goods in town. Your business is no different.

Expand, by all means, but anchor each new service or product firmly to your core value proposition to ensure it strengthens, not weakens, your business promise.

Sticking to your core doesn't mean stagnation, but rather it embodies an unshakeable understanding of your unique market offering and a commitment to relentless improvement within that domain. It's complementing the heirloom tomatoes with handpicked basil — augmenting without overshadowing. This steadfast focus on your core proposition will not only deepen customer trust but will set you up as the go-to expert, the thought leader in your niche. After all, when you weave your value proposition into every thread of the customer experience, you don't just serve; you resonate, inspire, and become a part of your customer's story.

Chapter 9:
Keeping It in the Family

Strolling through the aisles of my family's grocery store, watching my parents interact with customers, I learned a fundamental truth that has stuck with me throughout my career: a family business doesn't just serve its members; it extends that feeling of belonging to each employee and customer. When you run your business like a family, every interaction becomes more personal, every service becomes a matter of pride, and your team operates like a tight-knit unit that can weather any storm. You see, 'keeping it in the family' isn't about nepotism; it's about fostering a culture where loyalty, dedication, and commitment are the norm.

The strength of a family business lies not just in its heritage, but in the ability to *lead by example.* Leaders in any successful organization must do more than bark orders from a high-rise office; they must walk the walk. This means standing shoulder to shoulder with your team, understanding their challenges, and guiding them by your own actions. It's about showing up day in and day out, demonstrating your investment in the company's values, and inspiring your employees by your steadfast dedication. This approach not only earns respect, but it also instills a sense of shared mission that can propel a company to remarkable achievements.

As important as leadership is, it's just as vital to **recognize and reward** the people who keep the wheels of your business turning. I learned from watching my folks behind the register that a simple 'thank you' or an unexpected bonus can transform an average employee into a superstar. It's not so much about the monetary value but the acknowledgment of effort and the affirmation that their contribution makes a difference. This kind of recognition builds loyalty and fosters a work environment that's buzzing with motivation and enthusiasm.

In a family, core values are passed down like cherished heirlooms, and the same should be true for your business. The principles that my parents upheld—integrity, hard work, customer-first mentality—were absorbed by our staff and, in turn, felt by our customers. Embedding your core values in every aspect of the business demonstrates that you're not just in it for short-term gains but are cultivating a legacy of excellence and trust.

Let's face it, when you treat your business like a family, you create an ecosystem where each member doesn't just work for a paycheck but supports a shared vision. They stand together through thick and thin, celebrate each other's successes, and strive for a collective goal. Bringing your 'family' along for the journey not only enriches the work life for your team but ensures customers keep coming back, knowing they're treated as part of that very family. So, take a look around you—your employees, your colleagues, they're your extended family. Keep them close, treat them right, and together, you'll take your business to unparalleled heights.

Leadership Walks the Walk Ingrained in the atmosphere of a thriving family-owned grocery store is the palpable presence of leadership that's not afraid to roll up its sleeves. In our store, leaders didn't just manage from behind a desk. They were on the floor, stocking shelves, chatting with customers, and even bagging groceries. This hands-on approach sent a clear message: if it's important to the customer, it's important to us, no matter what level we're at within the organization. This kind of authentic, visible leadership commitment is a cornerstone for creating an exceptional customer experience.

Imagine a CEO who doesn't just talk about customer service but shows up unannounced at different locations to engage with both employees and customers alike. It's leadership by example that resonates at every level of the company. When leaders exemplify the values they preach, it builds trust and fosters an environment where employees feel empowered to go above and beyond because they know their leaders would do the same. It's about creating a culture where the norm is to 'walk the walk', and it starts with leaders who don't just pass down orders but are willing to lead the charge.

This active approach transcends the boundaries of traditional management and veers into the realm of impassioned stewardship. Leaders in any business setting can adopt this principle. If you want your team to prioritize customer satisfaction, let them see you prioritize it. Respond to a service call, handle a tricky customer situation, and embed yourself in the nitty-gritty of daily operations. Such actions galvanize your team to mirror that level of dedication. They signal that there's no task beneath anyone and that each role is vital to delivering that exceptional experience our family's grocery store—and your business—strives for every day.

Rewarding the Employees As we venture further into the fabric of what makes a business not just survive, but truly thrive, it's imperative to recognize a cornerstone that often acts as the backbone of success: the employees. In the intimate setting of a family grocery store, it's crystal clear that every team member plays an instrumental role in creating an exceptional customer experience. To enable this, a reward system must be in place that not only acknowledges effort but also cultivates a culture of ownership and pride.

In essence, rewarding employees isn't solely about monetary bonuses or raises - though they can certainly be part of it. It's about creating an environment where people feel valued, seen, and connected to the broader mission of the business. Employees should be rewarded for embodying the core values of the company, for going the extra mile for a customer or for their collaboration and innovation when working in a team. Whether it's through non-traditional perks, public recognitions, professional growth opportunities, or team celebrations, these gestures resonate deeply, reinforcing the commitment to the team and, by extension, to your customers.

It's also about ensuring that recognition happens regularly and authentically. Random acts of appreciation, like handwritten thank you notes or impromptu days off, can be incredibly powerful. The key is to make sure that these are not one-offs, but part of a sustained effort that employees can rely on and look forward to. Employees who feel they're rewarded for their hard work are more likely to put forth their best effort every day, leading to a virtuous cycle of positivity and productivity. This doesn't just build a better work environment; it creates a loyal, passionate workforce that will carry forward the legacy of exceptional customer service, today and into the future.

Core Values Carried Over In the heart of every thriving business are core values that act as the bedrock for their success; these values are the torchbearers from the past that keep the future illuminated. Picture the family-owned grocery store, where trust, reliability, and personal service aren't just slogans—they're a way of life. These values don't just apply in the retail grocery space; they are universally transferrable and absolutely critical when creating an exceptional customer experience in any sector. It's about taking those old school principles—the care, the diligence, the willingness to go the extra mile—and entwining them with the bigger business tapestry of today.

Imagine each interaction with a customer is like handing over a fresh loaf of bread right from the oven—this embodies the essence of great service. It's that personal touch, the extra attention to detail, an understanding of the customer's needs, which sets a business apart from the rest. These values must carry over into modern practice, irrespective of technology or scale. By holding onto the ethos of 'The Customer Comes First', 'Respect and Honesty', and 'Quality Service', leaders maintain a culture that not only values but reveres the standards set by the bygone era of mom-and-pop shops.

In today's fast-paced world, where everything is about instant gratification, the question to ponder is how to sustain the charm and the warmth of personalized service. Persistence is key here. It is paramount, as leaders, to engrain these core values in every aspect of the organization, from top management down to frontline employees. It's not about nostalgia; it's about drawing from a rich heritage of customer service that forms the very DNA of an exceptional business. When these values carry over, they don't just build brands; they build legacies—ones that outlast marketing campaigns and trends, resonating deeply with customers, generation after generation.

Chapter 10:
When the Lights Go Out —
Crisis Management and Recovery

Imagine the freezers at your local grocery store suddenly stop working. The ice cream starts to melt, the meat begins to thaw, and time is ticking. This, in essence, is crisis management for you. It's not about preventing the inevitable breakdowns or blackouts, because, let's face it, they'll happen. It's about the hustle that follows. In this chapter, we immerse ourselves in the fast-paced world of bouncing back when things go south because the real test of our mettle shines brightest when the lights go out.

Invariably, every business, family-owned or not, is going to face crises. But here's where core principles are more than just nice quotes on the wall — they're lifelines. Corner grocery store principle number five isn't about literal aisles; it's about clearing paths through obstacles and ensuring there's a way to keep serving customers, come what may. It's about transparency with your team, rallying the troops, and showing that your doors — whether physical or virtual — remain open for business and ready to navigate through the storm.

Crisis management requires a blend of swift action, clear communication, and a robust pre-planned recovery strategy. Like a grocery store facing an unexpected power outage, businesses need to keep a cool head and a contingency plan ready. You can't afford to waste a minute because customers rely on you, and every moment that passes is a trust chip slipping away. You have to be the steady hand guiding your panicked team and assure your customers that you're capable of handling the heat in the kitchen.

Now, let's talk recovery. When the dust settles, it's the moment to recalibrate and rise, and it's not just about restoration. It's a prime opportunity to learn, to improve, and to prevent the same crisis from recurring. Just like a grocery clerk quickly restocks the shelves after they've been cleared, ensuring that every item returns better placed and products are fresh, a business should review every angle of the incident with a magnifying glass. It's crucial to dissect the crisis while it's still fresh on your mind—a true recovery is also an upgrade.

Moreover, recovering from a crisis is also a chance to reaffirm your commitment to your customers. It's a stage where you can infuse resilience, not just into your operations, but into the very heart of your brand's story. Your customers want to see that not only can you face adversity, but you can emerge stronger, smarter, and with a renewed focus on their needs. When the lights come back on, it's your cue to shine brighter than before, reassuring your patrons that no matter what happens, they can count on you to deliver an exceptional experience every single time.

CORNER GROCERY STORE PRINCIPLE #5:

"Keep the Aisles Clear and the Doors Open" pivots on resilience, urging leaders to ensure operational agility to keep the business thriving no matter what challenges roll down the aisles.

This principle is more than just a directive for keeping physical pathways free of clutter; it's a philosophy that ensures customers always have a way to what they need. Just like in a grocery store where blocked aisles can frustrate shoppers and impede sales, obstacles in business operations can prevent customers from receiving the service they're after. Think of every process in your organization as an aisle leading to the treasure—the customer's satisfaction. Your goal? Keep that path clear. Remove unnecessary bureaucracy, streamline your systems, and offer clear guidance so that customers can move swiftly from desire to fulfillment.

Moreover, opening your doors wide implies accessibility and a welcoming atmosphere. Is your customer service always reachable? Can your clients navigate your services as easily as one would stroll down a spacious, well-signed grocery aisle? Make sure you're not just physically available, but that you're emotionally and cognitively accessible too. When customers feel they are heard and understood, when they're met with a 'can-do' attitude and a willingness to go the extra mile, they're more likely to return. After all, an open door not only invites existing customers to stay but beckons to potential patrons as well.

Critically, keeping aisles clear and doors open extends beyond the customer experience to your team dynamics. Team members must collaborate without friction, just like customers navigate our aisles. Encourage open communication, clear role expectations, and the prompt clearing of any internal roadblocks. Managers should inspire this flow, cultivating an environment where employees are equipped to deliver on the promise of exceptional service. When internal pathways are free of obstructions, your team can focus on what truly matters—the customer. Remember, an accessible and inviting atmosphere for your team translates into the customer's experience. To excel in service, ensure every pathway, both literal and figurative, in your environment supports a smooth, unobstructed journey to success.

Chapter 11:
Seasonal Changes — Adapting and Innovating with the Times

As we transition from the nuts and bolts of crisis management, let's turn to the rhythm of change and the music of innovation that must play in the background of every high-performing business. In my family's grocery store, the shift in seasons wasn't just about swapping out the produce; it was a front-row seat to understanding our customer's evolving needs and wants. It's the same in any business; as the seasons change, so do the opportunities to connect with your customers.

Imagine walking into the store as the first leaves of fall begin to carpet the sidewalk — suddenly, there's an aroma of cinnamon and apples wafting through the air, pumpkins are piled high, and the once vibrant rows of summer berries have been replaced by an avalanche of oranges and yellows. This wasn't just about celebrating autumn; it was a sign that we were in tune with our customers' lives. It's a dance every business must learn — the steps involve listening, anticipating, and then artfully responding to the rhythm of your customer's changing needs.

Now, let's fast-forward to the digital age, where seasons don't just change outside our windows but within the scrolling feeds of social media and the trending bars of the internet. Staying relevant isn't just about swapping out products; it's about breathing the same cultural air as your customers. What are they tweeting about? What memes are making them laugh? What challenges are they facing as the year unfolds? Understanding these layers allows us to innovate with products, services, and marketing in ways that resonate deeply.

The core principle here, which I like to call "Every Season Has Its Reason," is a pledge to adaptability. It's what keeps a business fresh and personal, no matter its size. Being adaptable doesn't mean you're aimlessly chasing after every new trend; it's about discerning which waves are worth catching. This selective innovation ensures that every change hits close to home for your customers, making them feel seen and understood. We can't fight the waves of change, but we can definitely learn to surf them.

In conclusion, the message is straightforward but profound. As you lead your teams and businesses into the future, make sure your sails are ready to catch the winds of change. Stay alert, stay agile, and most importantly, stay connected to the heartbeat of your customers. That way, you won't just weather the seasonal changes; you'll be pioneering the path forward, leaving a bouquet of blossoming innovations in your wake.

CORNER GROCERY STORE PRINCIPLE #6:

"Every Season Has Its Reason: Adaptability Is Key" In the ever-shifting landscape of customer needs, "Every Season Has Its Reason: Adaptability Is Key" embodies the spirit of innovation and flexibility that ensures we not only anticipate changes but also embrace them to stay ahead of the curve.

If there's one thing a neighborhood grocery store knows, it's how the seasons impact what's on the shelves and in the hearts of customers. Consider how the crisp fall air ushers in pumpkins and warm apple cider, or how summer beckons for cool, juicy watermelon slices. Each season brings new demands; each phase of life requires a different approach. Approach your business with the same mindset. Seize the seasonal shifts in the market as opportunities to cater to evolving needs and preferences. After all, staying relevant isn't about being stagnant—it's about being as adaptable as the trees shedding leaves to prepare for winter.

Think of your business strategy as you would the rich tapestry of nature's cycles. In spring, new products blossom, brimming with possibility. As the summer heat intensifies, so does the competition, urging you to find innovative ways to stay cool under pressure. When autumn's harvest comes around, it's a time to reap what you've sown, to showcase the fruitful outcomes of diligent, adaptive work. And winter? That's when you cozy up with your customers, providing that warm, comforting service that they'll return for year-round. In the corporate realm, this means continuously evolving your service offerings, staying ahead of trends, and ensuring you have the right technology and tools to thrive in any season.

Let's face it, execs and leaders, your customers are chameleons, and they expect you to be one too. They're always changing, their needs diversifying as quickly as the seasons pass. Adaptability is not just a strategy; it's a survival trait. So, pivot with purpose, whether that means revamping your loyalty programs to match customer expectations or transforming the service delivery model to meet the new digital age head-on. Remember, the goal isn't just to weather the storms—it's to dance in the rain and harness the energy of the lightning. Adapt with intention, grip the helm with confidence, and watch your business flourish, no matter the season.

Chapter 12:
The Secret Recipe – Sustaining Success Through Community Connection

So we've navigated the aisles, restocked the shelves, and considered every season's offerings. Now, let's blend these learnings into a secret recipe—a formula that binds business success to the soul of the community. Understand that community connection isn't just about geography; it's the invisible web of interactions, support, and shared values that form the foundation of your customer experience. Embrace this, and you're not just another store on the block; you become a cherished gathering spot. That's the nature of our corner grocery store: a central hub where everyone feels like they're part of something bigger. This is where sustainability lies, not just in environmental terms, but in ensuring that your business thrives year after year.

In fostering this vital connection, remember that every interaction counts, and each one is an opportunity to extend your roots deeper into the community soil. It's not simply about transactions; it's about the lasting impression you leave. It's about the smiles, the "Good morning!" banter, and the "How's your family?" follow-ups. This kind of engagement is priceless. It turns customers into advocates, and passersby into loyal patrons. You might not see instant revenue spikes from such efforts, but the gradual buildup of trust and goodwill is like a savings account that compounds interest exponentially in the form of customer loyalty.

Weaving the community into the tapestry of your business means showing up where it matters. Sponsor that local baseball team, participate in charity events, or host a community day. Let your presence signal a commitment to more than just profits, but to the health, well-being, and growth of the area you serve. It's a gesture that says you're here to stay and that you don't just take from the community—you give back. As you invest in these relationships, your business becomes a cherished community pillar, one that stands resilient even as economic winds shift and trends come and go.

And it's not enough to simply show up and smile. Authenticity is the heart of the matter. In our family store, that meant knowing the names of the kids who came in to buy candy after school and remembering the favorite bread of the elderly gentleman down the street. In your business, it could mean sending a follow-up note after a significant purchase or checking in with a customer who hasn't been around in a while. It's the warmth of genuine concern and interest that sparks a connection, shining through every policy and service you offer.

Ultimately, the secret to enduring success serves as the seventh Corner Grocery Store Principle: the secret ingredient is always love. When your community is sure they're not just faces in the customer line but valued members of your business family, they'll reward you with dedication and support. Now, that's a recipe worth perfecting, as it's the flavor of success that everyone can savor for generations to come.

CORNER GROCERY STORE PRINCIPLE #7:

"The Secret Ingredient Is Always Love" embodies the warmth and genuine care that elevates a simple transaction into a meaningful interaction, reminding us that infusing our services with a dash of heartfelt connection can transform client relations and create enduring loyalty.

In the throes of daily transactions, amidst the hustle and excitement of sealing deals and cultivating new business avenues, there's a critical ingredient that should never be forgotten: Love. At the heart of every meaningful customer interaction, there's a genuine warmth and caring that sets remarkable businesses apart. Think about it – when a customer feels genuinely cared for, not just as another sale but as a valued part of your business family, they're more likely to return, time and time again.

Love isn't just a feeling; it's a practice. It's the active decision to listen wholeheartedly, to act with empathy, and to go above and beyond to solve someone's problem. Within the walls of my family's grocery store, we knew our regulars' names, their families, and what they liked. This level of care may seem daunting to implement on a larger scale, but it's the bridge between a transaction and a relationship. When customers know they are loved, they don't just bring their wallets to your store; they bring their trust, loyalty, and they rave about their experience to others, becoming a beacon for your brand.

So how do we sprinkle this secret ingredient into every business interaction? Start with your internal culture. Cultivate an environment where your team feels appreciated and empowered to spread love through their work. Encourage them to find moments to make a personal connection with customers, to treat every interaction not as a routine but as an opportunity to leave someone better than they found them. By embedding love into your corporate DNA, you create a ripple effect that resonates through every facet of your enterprise. At the end of the day, people may forget what exactly was said or done, but they will always remember how you made them feel – and love, that powerful, unifying force, is what they will remember most.

From Corner Store to Corporate — Carrying the Legacy Forward

As we close the cover on the journey from the cozy aisles of a family-run corner store to the expansive hallways of corporate enterprises, it's vital to pause and reflect on the essence of what makes a business transcend ordinary interactions to create an extraordinary customer experience. This is not just about transactions; it's about traditions, not mere exchanges but enduring connections. Every principle birthed from the humble beginnings of that neighborhood grocery is a building block for an exceptional legacy in any business you touch.

Remember that the presence of leadership is foundational. Like the ever-watchful eyes of a store owner, leaders in any corporate setting must be actively engaged and deeply invested in the daily ebb and flow of their business. Embrace the spirit of the deli counter — adaptability, personalization, and the flexibility to serve up solutions that are as unique as each individual who walks through your doors. Our ethos originates from the desire not just to meet needs, but to understand the person behind the purchase.

Let's not forget the delivery boy's tenacity, symbolizing the core value of 'do whatever it takes' to deliver the goods. And when paying for value at checkout serves as a reminder that our transactions are trust exchanges, each one is a pledge of quality and satisfaction. Like the steadfast delivery boy, in every role you hold, strive to leave an indelible mark of reliability and commitment. Into the corporate world, carry that cherished value of seeing every end as a setup for the next beginning, nurturing lifetimes of customer connection.

Through growth, change, and even crisis, hold fast to the principles that underpin both small family businesses and larger organizations. The ability to adapt, as evident by the changing seasons of the corner store, is indispensable in a corporate environment that is in constant flux. And, as we reminisce about 'keeping the aisles clear,' it's a metaphor for maintaining clarity of vision amidst inevitable challenges. It's this resolve to navigate disruptions with grace that fortifies a company's resilience.

Ultimately, the secret recipe that has woven its way through our narrative is simple yet profound: infuse every facet of your business with love. From corner store to corporate, it's the legacy of heartfelt service, resilient adaptability, and unwavering commitment that forms the quintessence of a thriving customer experience. This legacy is not just carried forward; it is expanded, enriched, and exemplified in the values and visions you instill in your team and your brand. Embrace these timeless principles and watch as they transform not just your approach to business, but also the lives of those you serve.

Appendix A: Implementing Corner Grocery Store Principles in Your Business

We've journeyed together through the rich aisles of wisdom from a humble corner grocery store, extracting timeless principles to infuse into your own business. These principles aren't just quaint reminders of simpler times; they're powerful strategies for delivering an exceptional customer experience that spells distinction and success in any industry. Now, let's roll up our sleeves and get practical about how to make these cornerstone principles work for you and your team.

First and foremost, it's about capturing that *family business mindset*. This isn't merely about being familial in your approach; it's a comprehensive attitude—one that encompasses presence, adaptability, commitment to service, and relentless pursuit of delivering value that keeps customers returning. To implement this mindset, you should involve yourself deeply with the daily operations of your business, just as the proprietor would at a family-owned grocery store. Can't expect to understand your customer's experience if you're not on the front lines witnessing it unfold.

Echoing Principle #1, leaders must not only be present but fully accountable for the customer experience. This means not just making decisions from an ivory tower but connecting with employees and customers alike. Leadership presence helps to build a culture where every team member understands the value they bring to the table and the impact they make. It's not enough to merely say you value service; show it through your actions every single day.

Next up, flex like the deli counter—able to switch from thick to thin without missing a beat Principle #2. Flexibility in this context doesn't simply mean bending to every customer's whim. It's about finding innovative ways to deliver value, personalizing your service, and adapting to the ever-changing demands of the market with agility and poise.

Then consider Principle #3, treating customers with the individual care they deserve. This isn't about literal fruits and vegetables; it's about recognizing the uniqueness of each customer and tailoring your approach. Some customers prefer the self-service route; others thrive on personal interaction. The skill lies in discerning these preferences and catering to them without compromising your service standards.

Principle #4 is all about delivery, and I'm not just talking about the physical act. Do whatever it takes to meet your customers' needs, whether that's literal doorstep delivery or going the extra mile in service. An 'own it' mentality must permeate through every level of your organization. When the entire team takes ownership, every customer interaction becomes an opportunity to excel and delight.

Never forget that every transaction is a moment of truth Principle #5. Crisis management isn't just about weathering the storm; it's about keeping your halls navigable and your doors opened wide, no matter what. Maintain clarity in your operations and communications, ensuring that even when things don't go as planned, you're poised for quick recovery and continuous service.

Change with the seasons Principle #6 and you'll stay relevant. Adaptability seems to be a recurring theme, right? That's because it's crucial for long-term success. Just as grocery stores shift their offerings with the seasons, be proactive in anticipating and leading change within your industry. Adapt before you're forced to, pivot when necessary, and always stay true to the core value that defines you.

And lastly, never underestimate the power of love, the secret ingredient Principle #7. Injecting love and genuine care into every facet of your business can transform transactions into relationships and single purchases into lifetime loyalty.

Implementing these corner grocery store principles may not happen overnight. It involves a conscious, consistent effort across the board. Involve your team, set clear expectations, and keep the dialogue open about how these principles can translate into daily operations. Reward team members who embody these values, listen actively to customer feedback, and always keep an eye on how to refine your service.

Your business, regardless of its size or industry, can harness the heartwarming, effective essence of the corner grocery store. Remember, it's the little things done exceptionally well that create a customer experience that's not just satisfactory, but remarkable.

THE SEVEN CORNER GROCERY STORE PRINCIPLES

CORNER GROCERY STORE PRINCIPLE #1
"Leaders Must Be Present and Accounted For"

CORNER GROCERY STORE PRINCIPLE #2
"Thick or Thin, Flexibility Is In"

CORNER GROCERY STORE PRINCIPLE #3
"Treat Your Customer Like a Fruit or Vegetable. Just Make Sure You Know the Difference"

CORNER GROCERY STORE PRINCIPLE #4
"Do Whatever It Takes to Deliver the Goods"

CORNER GROCERY STORE PRINCIPLE #5
"Keep the Aisles Clear and the Doors Open"

CORNER GROCERY STORE PRINCIPLE #6
"Every Season Has Its Reason: Adaptability Is Key"

CORNER GROCERY STORE PRINCIPLE #7
"The Secret Ingredient Is Always Love"

Appendix B: Acknowledgments

As we close the last page on the insights and stories that have peppered these chapters like the well-loved spices of a family recipe, I'm struck by the overwhelming sense of gratitude that bubbles up. This book isn't just bound pages of text; it's a narrative steeped in the flavors of countless contributions, rich experiences, and steadfast support. It crystallizes lessons from the corner grocery that fed not just the belly, but the soul of a community. So, let's shine a spotlight on those remarkable people who've made this journey far more than I could've walked alone.

I'm indebted first and foremost to my family, the original cast of my corner grocery playbook. Running the aisles, stocking the shelves – everything I've learned about the heart of customer service started with those early memories. Your unconditional love and belief in hard work and integrity have been the cornerstones of this endeavor, and for that, I thank you from the bottom of my heart.

To my mentors, those sagacious guides who've been both compass and anchor throughout this voyage, your wisdom has been invaluable. You taught me to see both the forest and the trees, to understand that the best leaders are also listeners, eternally curious and humble in their pursuit of excellence. Without your patience and insights, these pages would be barren.

Let's not forget the tireless teams I've had the fortune to lead and learn from. You are the unsung heroes, the customer service warriors who embody the spirit of what we stand for. Your dedication keeps the engine of our enterprise roaring, your passion keeps our purpose aflame. You've shown that the principles of the corner grocery don't just live in the past, they're alive and well, driving us toward a future we shape together.

To my peers in the business community, both competitors and collaborators, thank you for continually pushing the boundaries of what's possible. Thank you for the camaraderie, the shared vision, and the healthy challenge that reminds us that we're part of a greater ecosystem, striving to deliver an exceptional customer experience.

Last, but certainly not least, I extend my gratitude to you, the readers. Your commitment to enriching your organizations, to bringing the ethos of a family-owned business into your corporate cultures, inspires a brighter future for all who cross your path.

Together, we've journeyed from the tactile memory of our neighborhood grocery, with its personal touch and close-knit community, to an expanse where these principles find new life in the wider world of business. Let's continue to carry this legacy forward, nurturing an exceptional customer experience that transcends the transaction and becomes a lasting tradition.

Made in the USA
Monee, IL
05 March 2025